I0446028

The Shadows Could Not Reach Her

Kristin Lansing (-Stoeffler)

Ice Cube Press, LLC
North Liberty, Iowa, USA

The Shadows Could Not Reach Her

Copyright ©2024 Kristin Lansing (-Stoeffler)

First Edition

Isbn 9781948509541

Library of Congress Control Number: 2024934848

Ice Cube Press, LLC (Est. 1991)
1180 Hauer Drive, North Liberty, Iowa 52317
www.icecubepress.com steve@icecubepress.com

The paper used in this publication meets the minimum requirements of the American National Standard for Information Sciences—Permanence of Paper for Printed Library Materials, ANSI Z39.48-1992.

Made with recycled paper.

Manufactured in USA

Sullivan!
Poseybelle!
Fritz!
My constellation.
Brilliant, steady, and strong.

PreRAMBLE

The journey from expression to impression is mutable and beautiful. The process of expression is sparked by a seed of inspiration, rooted deeply. Created as a catharsis, a cure, a celebration—then shared. Freed, given, released for interpretation, impression on a heart, a soul. Without control. These creations will not travel this journey alone, words are their companions. Each painting has stories, essays, and poems. Veiled and inviting. Honest and owned. Stories not told, but hinted by truths embedded. Expression inviting impression. The making of meaning.

INTRODUCTION

Warm light bathed the gloss of our table and barely spilled beyond our conversation, held closely as not to disturb or intrigue.

As friends we took shelter here from the creeping cool of autumn that was beginning to seep into the early evenings, making things move quickly, people move quickly, thoughts move quickly. A rush to escape the cooling realities that arise from the quiet and still.

We were welcomed here with the warmth of downlit tables, art, and intellectual conversations hushed between sips of steeping tea and coffee and friends.

At our table my questioning was sincere, "What do you think of when you see this painting?"

It wasn't a fair question. The answer was loaded. I had pushed her to unease and I did it on purpose. I tried not to smile. She wanted to have the right answer. She always had the right answer. Brilliant thinker and inspiring friend she had paved a speeded and rewarding path out of right answers. There was no right answer this time and I knew it.

She leaned back to allow and reserve more space for thought and inspiration for the right answer. She stared thoughtfully, without looking, at the warm glow and predictable patterns of the wooden table, but was seeing only her thoughts.

"I see," she stated eventually with the resolution of someone who had determined a solution to submit, "a sunset, and light that has been filtered through many layers of atmosphere and refracted to create many colors."

I broke into a knowing giddy smile and leaned-in with appreciation and glee. "I love that that is your answer! Of course it is your answer! I would not have thought of it!"

It was calculated and correct and precise. It was a deduction of logic and facts. It was science and it was sincere. It was what she saw when she looked at the painting. It was what she thought when she saw it. It was her analysis, but not her impression, and that was the whole point.

"Would you want to know what it means—the painting? I mean, would you want to know what I was thinking when I painted it? If you knew, would that change what you saw?"

I had been to the gallery and had seen the paintings with their tags and titles and descriptions. I didn't want to read them. I didn't want to know what the artist was thinking. I didn't want to know what the artist was feeling. I didn't want the context, I wanted the experience of my own impression. I wanted to make my own meaning. I wanted the meaning to be my own.

She wanted the context. She wanted the right answers. She wanted a frame and foundation to inform the audience and I didn't understand.

For my work I knew my journey. The process was the stillness that had allowed for the silence to hear the unheard and see the unseen. To know the deep and quiet meaning. To find equilibrium between my path and the distance that spanned my past and my future. My balance. My connection between what was and what was to come.

Nearly finished I would step back and steep in the image. Why those clouds? Why those clouds that way? Why those colors? Why those layers? Why that distance? And the answer would take form with the deep ache of truth. Inconvenient truths. Latent truths unearthed and washed clean. Celebrated truths. Triumphant truths. Not scars, but maps of my evolution. Evidence of becoming. Honest and owned.

What value would these truths be to her? Details to decipher the right answer? A story to absolve her of creating her own? A map to guide her to a determined destination? A solution for serendipity?

Could I share without taking?

The journey is not the destination. Each holds its own space and its own place. Together they create completeness. She could have both, separately, and create her own connections.

I spun my spoon around the porcelain rim above the dropping depths of my now shallow pool of tea. I returned to my sincere questioning, staring without looking, and trying again not to smile. The answers hidden in my thoughtful gaze, and not yet to be shared.

"So that is what you think when you see the painting, but what do you feel?"

The question was intrusive and again unfair.

There was no right answer and I knew it.

There was no wrong answer either, and that was the whole point.

THIS IS YOUR JOURNEY

Each painting in this book has a poem or an essay, or both.

These are all included in no particular order to allow you to make your own journey of impression while sharing my own. To give without taking.

Each painting is followed by space to allow you to establish your own connection and capture your own impression.

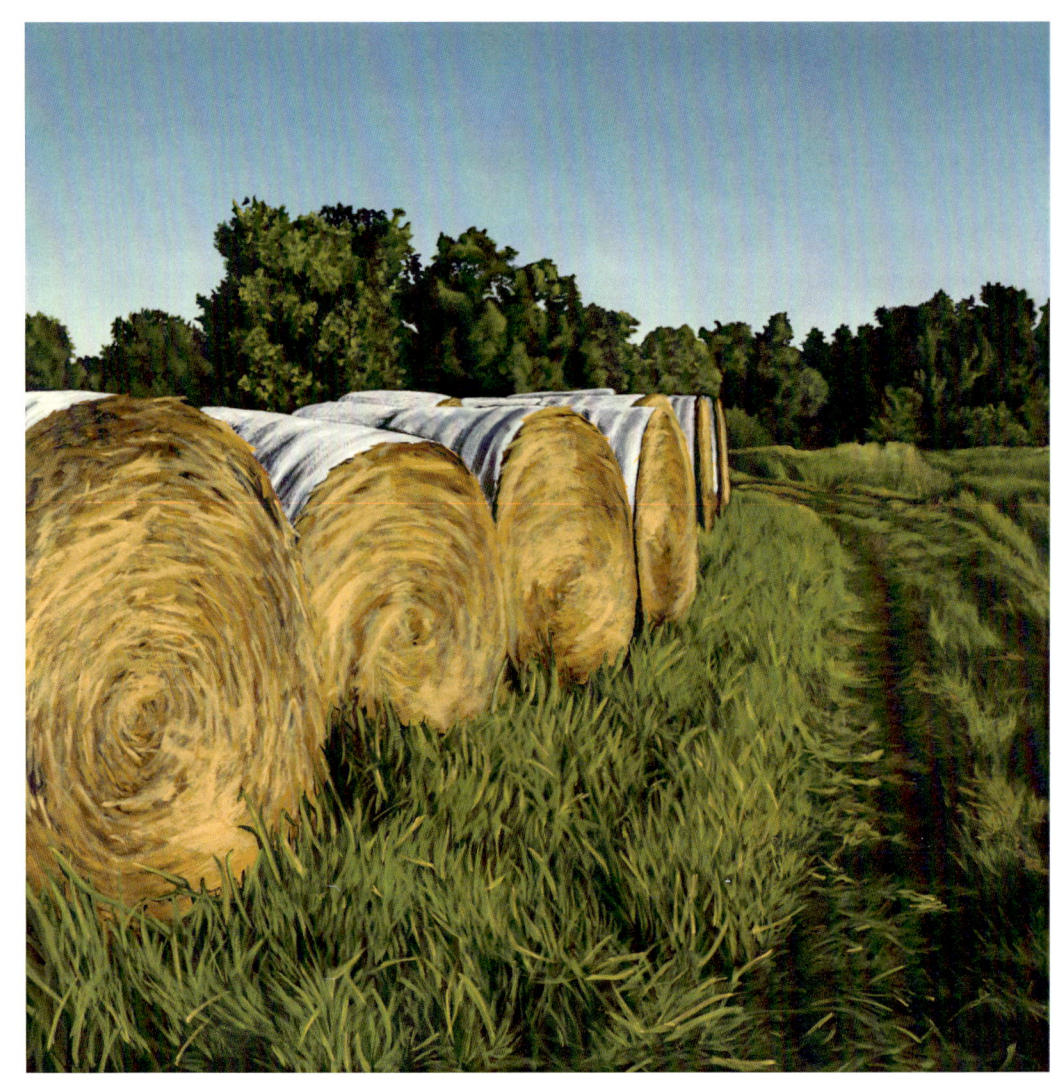

Painting 1

Painting 1: Impressions

ESSAY 1 (¼)

There it was. Looming in the corner. I had been avoiding it for weeks or months with lame justifications about being too busy.

It was time to move forward. I was stalled out. I had started this work months earlier and actually painted another painting in the meantime, having displaced it from the easel with empty promises to myself about finishing it later and excuses for not returning. With the newest work, a beautiful work, off the easel and on to the next stage of its journey I was ultimately faced with the guilt of continuing to actively avoid this piece by going out to buy a new canvas. It felt like quitting. I should be able to move forward with this piece. It was the church where I got married.

For days I had gotten up early and driven the opposite direction of my work to catch the church in the morning sunrise so that maybe the light would be right. Surely it would be right. I would leave work early when the sky was just perfect. The blue was just perfect. The clouds were just perfect. Yet nothing.

Walk up the road this way. Down the road that way. Cross the road. Stand in the ditch with the tall grasses. Wade through the tall grasses, through shoulder high grasses, to the other side. Cars passing slowly and wondering.

I ended up with an elaborate collection of uncomfortable images, brow furrowing images. But I was going to paint them anyway. I picked one and dedicated a canvas to it. Easel ready. Brushes ready. Paint ready. Sketch points mapped. Blue mixed, I built the sky, perfect and smooth. Perfect. Almost too easy this time, definitely a good sign. I mapped my points and negotiated the structure by the horizon. The structure stood in place, heavy, black and empty. Imposing on the perfect blue sky. In my mind I kept calling it a structure. A soulful relic from my past. Trying to fall in love with it, the love I thought I should have for it.

The structure sat for days. The days turned into weeks and I needed to paint. Two paintings made their way onto and off the easel and I was left again, months later, with my unfinished business. On the easel again. Waiting to be finished. The structure.

I grew up catholic, at the crossroads of German and Irish catholic families. My Irish grandma was an orphan, the result of a time when illness and the economy could wreak havoc on a society ill-prepared for such devastating deviations from the American Dream. Family was everything. Religion was a constant. Christian ministries were the last hope for many depression era widows unable to provide for their families. That's hard to reconcile, I'm sure, as my grandma still remembered her own father taking her to the orphanage and telling her he would be back. "He never came back." She was raised by the nuns and the church.

My German family practiced the faith at the crossroads of love and judgment. Heavy on both.

A structure can be a home, but not a haven.

POEM 1

So bright
So white
Definition dissolved
Boundaries denied
They disappeared within themselves
Which wasn't the truth
Light collected to capacity
Fully saturated
Completely
Impossibly
White
Blooming from a desperate darkness
Grey upon grey
Allowed only to form heavy blankets
Woven and stitched to slowly slip across a sky
Gazing only upon the bones of sleeping trees
Creatures hidden
To bloom
Tall, reaching plumes
Stretching and expanding from a stifled state
To fill the sky
Unfurled by warmth
To gaze again
Upon the greens

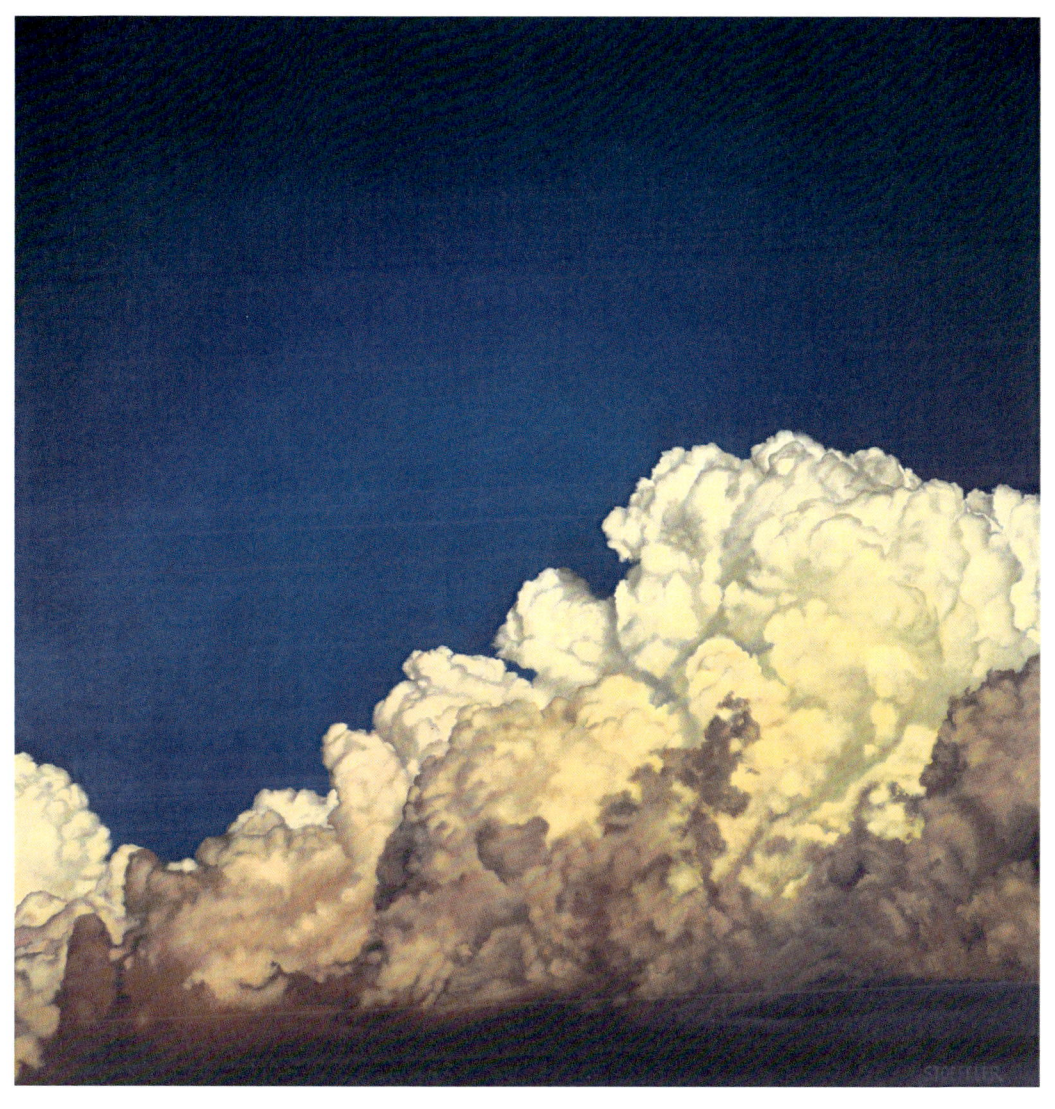

Painting 2

Painting 2: Impressions

ESSAY 2

The room with the leaded glass windows that faced the road also faced the sunrise. The room was glowing and before I even opened my eyes I could feel it. The day had started. It had not waited, it was going on without me and I could feel it. Pulling me out of bed, groggy in leggings and wool socks. I could smell coffee and hear muffled conversation through the heavy wooden door to the kitchen that wouldn't close tightly, stuck as if it was too sturdy, stubborn, and rough for even the frame it was designed to fit. I pulled on a stocking cap and old heavy wool shirt. I slipped through the kitchen stealing a glimpse through the window of the glittering grass in the pasture punctuated with bold black cows. Without stopping I poured some coffee into my mug while moving quickly past the morning greetings and out to the still-shadowy and cool porch to slip my oversized wool socks into my oversized rubber boots and escape out the back door, without stopping, balancing coffee and camera and pulling the door closed behind me. No questions, no companions, just the morning and me. Skipping the acknowledgment of myself and my relations, myself and my obligations. I just wanted to belong to the morning today.

I steeped in the sunrise, feeling the heavy humid air holding a promise of heat for the day to come. Sun on my face and glittering in the cool dew all around me, sparkling like fallen stars from the night before. I wanted to stay out of my head today, I did not want to be grounded in me just yet, I wanted to dissolve and disappear into the sounds and spaces, my senses, ungrounded, untethered, glittering, glowing and fleeting.

My awkward boots, unsteady, slippery with dew, navigated the ruts and rocks carved into the lane leading to the crest of the hill pieces. I could feel the sun warm on my back. I didn't worry for the coffee spilling from my mug, but noted instead the patient and steady steam rolling from the cool hollows to greet the day along with me, also catching the sun on it's steady rise.

I had visited this spot the night before, at dusk, sun sinking, cool creeping and rising up with the steadily growing haunting howling, a frenzy brewing in the hollows. The coyotes running the bottoms along the river. Howls eerie, empty. The coyotes like this spot, the crest of the hill pieces, at dusk. To claim the advantage of a vantage point allowed by the row of hay bales lining the fence. I needed to make a guess about what the morning light might bring. I knew that the sun would meet me here in the morning and the thought alone filled me with warm anticipation against the chill rising with the haunting howls from the hollows.

Morning shined like a promise now. The full line of glowing bales beamed like a sunrise stretched across the crest of the hill pieces as promised. Glowing warm and so bright. Wet and warming in the sun. Heavy and earthy, and plentiful and sweet. I smiled at the fat blades of grass and hay cool and sparkling as they stuck and pulled, begging at my boots as I walked across the still green hayfield. The coolness again spilled from the dense darkness of the forest lining the fields and pooled low in the grasses still waiting for the sun. I was not waiting.

I stood with my boots rooted in the deep cool of earth and grass and turned myself to join the bales with the sun on our pale welcome faces, warm and glowing together now on the crest of the hill pieces. Too bright to even see. Blinging brightness to obscure everything, disappear and dissolve everything, leaving only warmth to make sense of. I did not need to make sense or senses of anything now, I needed only to shine, rooted and tethered and warm and bright.

ESSAY 3

Sometimes waking up feels like breaking. Like night is being torn away. The comfort of night, the quiet of night, the easy sameness of night. The serenity of familiar darkness.

The world is the same whether bathed in light or covered in a blanket of darkness. In darkness, though, its rough edges smoothed. It's harsh realities paused, it's dissonance hidden, uncomfortable truths obscured by the quiet, simple darkness of night.

When the realities are inconvenient the glow of day does not come softly.

The glow can break across the whole sky, changing everything, touching everything, expanding to cover everything. Uncontrolled, uncontained, unavoidable.

And daybreak comes without apology. It does not ask permission, it does not wait, it does not waver. It arrives. Expands. Unfurls, unveils, and reveals all that was obscured. Lays bare the reality of the day without hesitation or reservation or apology.

Diem. Honest and owned.

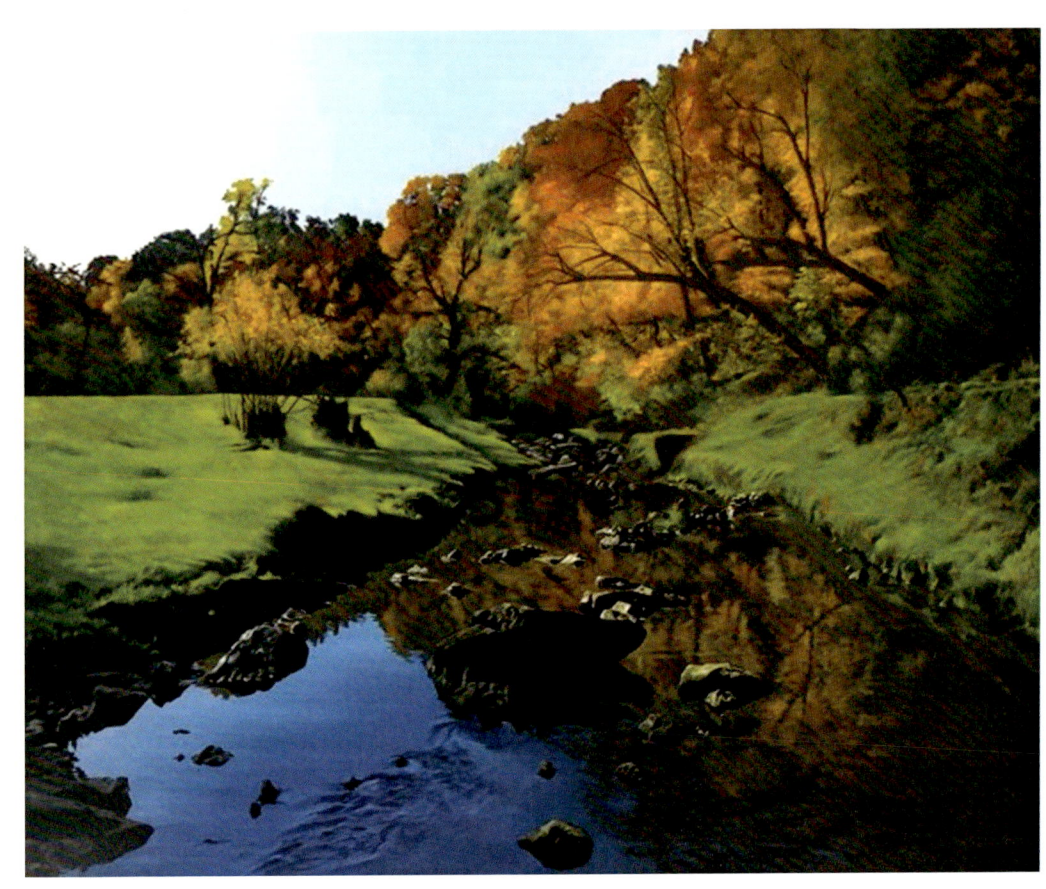

Painting 3

Painting 3: Impressions

ESSAY 4 (½)

We wove along the crest of the ridge that divided the rolling fields that dissolved into valleys and descended into towns. We were losing daylight, but winning one of the most expansive and awe-inspiring sunsets I had seen in a long time. There was so much sky to see from this ridge, as though the entirety of the sky was in view and the entirety of the sky was ablaze with color. This was no small sunset, this was the most enormous sunset I had ever seen. I was previously unaware that a sky could feel that immense and that a sunset could encompass so much of it. I ached to see all of it.

We dipped through the cool hollow, a shadowed canopy bowing to usher us through, gravel slipping beneath our tires, emerging to round the bend with the white farm house in view now. Dwarfed by this magnificent sky.

I jumped quickly down onto the cool grass and moved swiftly through the white picket gate, the tight metal spring pulling it sharply closed behind me. I steadied myself for the sound of it. Not daring to turn my eyes to the sky just yet, my sights set for the first hill piece gate. I strode quickly across the yard and through both red gates, closing heavy behind me. I wasn't worried. The cows were in the hollow. I hurried along the ruts of the lane that split the sidehill piece and the first hill piece. The cool air was rolling up from the hollows and I could smell it, spicy and green, feel it, pooling at my bare ankles. The grasses were catching the last gasp of golden that the sky had to offer, the deepest and heaviest gold. The grasses had little to glean from the corals and violets, their compliments. The earth was setting to sleep for the night. Turning in from a long spring day. Cooling, darkening, settling.

I was moving swiftly with anticipation, feeling what was surely above me. Halfway down the long gravel lane I stopped. I lifted my face to the sky. I opened my gaze to the brilliant sunset, so afraid that it would have faded. It hadn't. It stretched across the whole sky with absolute brilliance. Completely saturated in color. The whole sky. Completely saturated in color. The colors filled my soul completely to overflowing. I soaked them deep into me. I ached at the thought of them fading. I needed their depth and saturation to replenish me. I didn't want them to go. I wanted the sky to stay like that forever. My knowledge of the fleeting nature of day was tugging at my soul. I turned from the sky with intention and I didn't look back. I wanted to remember it as it was, unfaded.

I set my course for the dark horizon. My pace slower now, heavy now. Careful now to navigate my way home. Soon the moon would light my path. The owls would haunt the cool night air. The distance home would seem farther. The grasses colder, tugging at my bare ankles. The shadows deeper. The night air still, heavy, and dark. The path more cumbersome, more treacherous, and long. I kept my pace and let myself feel the creeping coolness, dissolving into the deepening darkness. Alone.

And then there were stars…

Twinkling, sparkling, bright and brilliant. Filling the deep and empty darkness of infinite indigo. Illuminating the intricacies and grandeur of these great depths. Shining above me, my timeless constant companions. Reminding me I was not alone, even at this great distance. My home would always be under this canopy of constellations, reminding me where I am. Who I am. Anywhere and everywhere. My wisdom for the journey forward. Brilliant, steady and strong.

ENTER THE SPRING:
PEOPLE ARE LIKE WHISKEY

Could anything be as predictably unpredictable and mutable as Midwest weather. Like variations full of variations. Iterations full of so many iterations. Gradients on gradients.

They talk about this being a perfect place to make whiskey. Spirits distilled from things the earth is willing to spare, poured into vessels that by their nature expand and contract with the seasons. Swelling and soaking and shrinking and squeezing. Pulling the liquid into the fibers of the wood and soaking them there until a shift in the wind and the tilt of the sun becomes pressing and the essence is expelled back to influence the rest until the wind should shift again. Over and over this process builds the contents to something different and unique to the seasons and conditions that created it. It is the essence of the seasons.

People are like whiskey. I could feel the seasons starting to swell within me today, like taking a deep breath in a general expansion of myself and my space, soaking up the new warmth and tilt of the sun. Swelling and soaking and shrinking and squeezing.

My sense of this coming expansion is inspiring and daunting. I will again begin to absorb feelings and thoughts and experiences. The green that has been hibernating within me aches to emerge from the waiting and reflecting, stewing and soaking, synthesizing the experiences endured in the previous season and preparing for the next. I feel this.

This metamorphosis is accompanied by an underlying sense of fear. A sense that I am so porous and my environment so ubiquitous that I might drown in its influence over me. Helpless to temper the power of these experiences being pulled into my fibers, knowing that I will become something different and unique to the seasons and conditions that cultivated me. I am a porous, joyous, essence of the seasons.

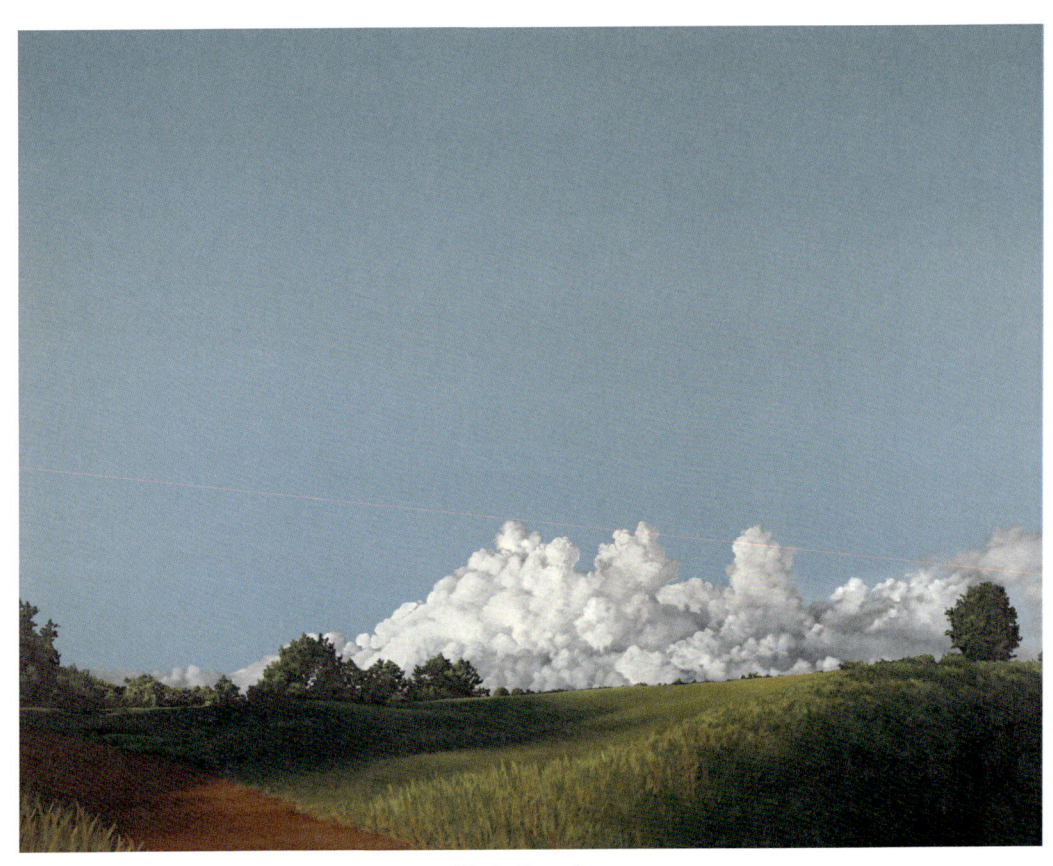

Painting 4

Painting 4: Impressions

ESSAY 5

I turned away from her. I placed her in a corner of my room and glanced at her from time to time as she wondered if I would return to tell her story. I didn't have the strength to listen. I turned her against the wall. She waited. For months she waited. Patient. Patiently holding her story, her secrets, her revelations from me. For me. Days and weeks and months went by and I kept watch over her while I solved the simple problems, listened to the simple stories that I had the strength to hear. Stories of triumph and calm, stories of understanding the value and depth of boundaries and distance. And when those stories were told she whispered to me if it was her time yet.

My soul felt whole and strong again. She had waited for me so patiently. I was ready to listen. I wanted to tell her story, every detail. It was hard to hear. She was very clear. Each attempt to work from a place of comfort and familiarity was denied. My techniques rejected. She wanted her own. Her story was unique and detailed and it needed its own cadence and colors. She would not compromise. I pushed myself far beyond my comfort level, building on learned techniques to give her what she needed. Heavy, single strokes of paint that could not be adjusted. One shot. One truth. No compromises. No fixes. No return. Wet paint on wet paint with a unique story told between them, without my intervention. Her surreal clarity enhanced by her faded friends, listening from a distance.

When her petals had shared their secrets, heavy and bold, she wanted her crown. She had earned it. Her spiraled florets were dizzying and seemed an impossible endeavor. Another. I did not even know how to start. But I did, and I knew she would let me know if I was wrong, and I was. So I tried again, and I knew she would let me know if I was wrong, and I was. I asked patiently and she said to start at the beginning and no matter what, listen to every detail, and trust in every decision. Don't ask, don't look, don't try to make sense until I've reached the end of the story. And I did. And I did.

She wears her crown heavy, earned, and honest. The weight of growth and knowing, struggle and sunshine. Patient with my insolence, my eagerness, my weakness, she taught me, told me, her story, secrets shared, revelations revealed, my lessons learned. To listen.

POEM 2

posts punctuating progress
punctuating boundaries
grasses, temper from tame
defining the distance
pulling perspective
All too far
grasses spilling sweet from shaded groves and gullies
grasses tangled, wild, woven, catching breezes
grasses tangled, wild, woven, whispering stories of sunshine
grasses tangled, wild, woven, hush the sun from posts and bales
grasses tangled, wild, woven, break the sun to scattered beams
grasses tangled, wild, woven, resilient
grasses tangled, wild, woven, cling, support, bend for all, not to
break or fall
grasses tangled, wild, woven, unrushed and unruly
Then tempered
tamed
Tailored and trained to smooth the rolling terrain
Reveal the calm undulation
now quiet
sweet
grasses

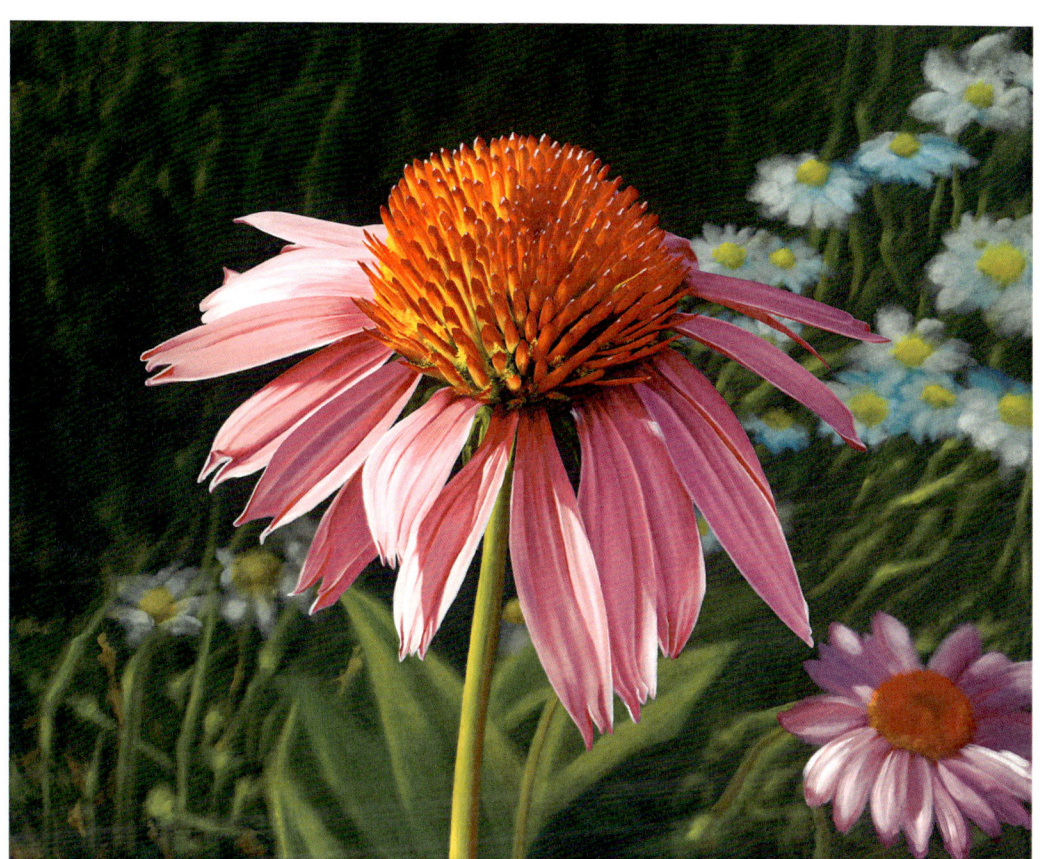

Painting 5

Painting 5: Impressions

ESSAY 1 (2/4)

Today, the work was just staring at me again and I was staring back in an uncomfortable negotiation. The dissonance was that it needed to be painted and I happened to be the painter. I was trying to mentally wrestle it to the ground, trying to find an angle through which I could generate some passion to fuel my desire to finish it. Start it.

Fine. Back to the structure. I'll start with grey and pull down to black where I need to and build up to white where I need to. Every little slat. Every shadowed frame. Every eve. Every warm white. Every demoted gray. The gray that hides under white, waiting. Okay, I can do this. Let's do this. I proceeded by, in stillness, building up the energy to slide off the bed and take my paintbrush in hand. The brushes are waiting. I can see the gray in my mind, the white, the palette. Time to move.

I can't do this.

I'm not doing this.

I'm done with this.

This painting doesn't want to be a church.

With this thought comes a swell of incredible lightness. I think it again. This painting doesn't want to be a church.

Even lighter now.

It wants to be something else.

Even brighter now.

It wants to be...and I waited for an image to emerge and committed myself to the idea that it would be the right image

...a skyscape.

Black again.

Back to black again.

Quickly.

Black over hours of planning. Black over months of waiting. Black over trying. Black over conjuring something that wasn't there. Black over mapped points. Black over an easy, perfect sky. Black to nothing.

A new beginning.

Black to indigo so deep it was brewed from the abyss. Black to indigo conjured from emptiness and hope. Black to indigo building to form a foundation to cultivate and hold a brilliant new beginning.

The skyscape.

POEM 3

Predictable cadence
rows and posts
Echoes
Planned and planted
Intentional distance
Allowances
Respites
Breaks and contrasts
Emphasize boundaries
Remove ambiguity
Emphasize truths
Define spaces
Allow for graces
Warm and kind
Deliverance from the cool racing shadows

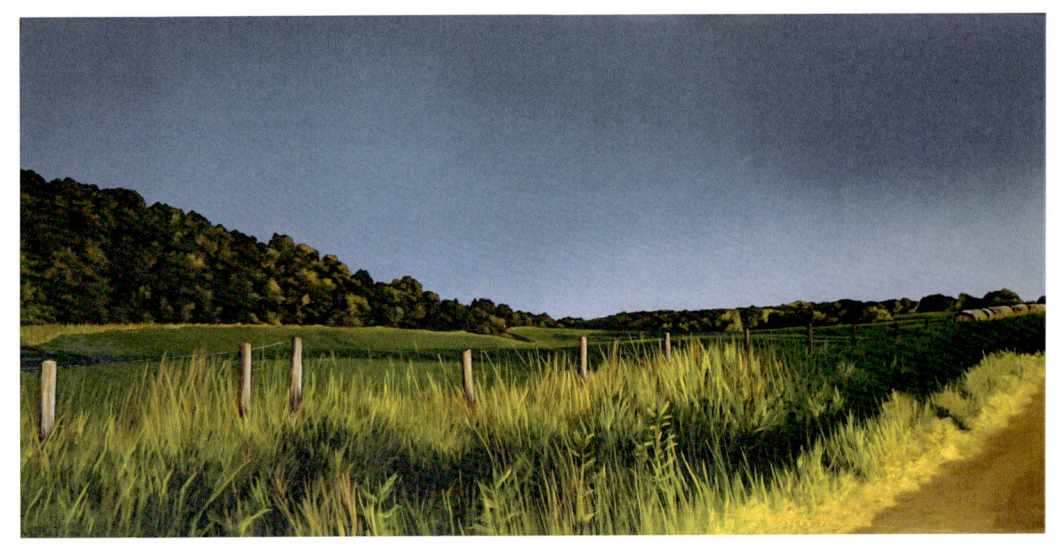

Painting 6

Painting 6: Impressions

ESSAY 6

In the evening the cool creeps and pools at bare ankles. Rolls from the hollows to settle between rows. The new green blades, dense and lush, with room to stretch straight to the sky between the tufted mounds.

The tufted mounds once formed the waves of a sea of greens. Brilliant and bold and soft. Easy and effortless. Calmly swaying with the breezes in a concert of solidarity and suppleness. Then cut. Raked to rows. Pointing the way to the horizon. Pointing the way home. Tufted mounds haphazard and scattered, untethered, stacked but strewn, and all within the spaces allowed between. Drying and cooling. Peaks glowing golden under the last warm rays of the day. The lows of the rows hiding from the sun, hugging the cool earth as soft, dusty lavenders and sage. Still spilling and stretching to touch the new blades, sharp, bold green blades. Hopeful and glowing, illuminated with the last sparks of sunlight. Tethered, still, to the dark cool earth below.

BELOW THE GLOW:
RESENTMENT AND CONTEMPT AS A PROXY FOR GUILT

I push charcoal and white lighter, and lighter, and lighter, but they can never become bright white again. I don't want them to. I hope they don't. Sometimes this is like diving deep and swimming up to the surface, aching for the surface, but never reaching the surface. Sometimes this is like enveloping myself deep in my old worn grey comforter where light is unwelcome, to avoid the extremes and the brightness.

These are the clouds that fall below the direct remaining rays of the sun as it is sinking. They don't glow. They don't tower. They toil, churn, and build. I churn with them this week. Mired in churn, below the glow. I'm comfortable with them, we're friends today, it's nice, we are the same for now. I will paint them in so many shades of charcoal and white knowing that they are much more than that, but this first. Charcoal and white. Later a wash in shades of coral, to become deep undulating shades of coral. But first this. Charcoal and white. They will never be coral until they are first charcoal and white. The coral would go unnoticed without the charcoal and white, but now, a canvas in their path to full diffusion. A touchstone before they disappear into the ether.

I've been waiting for these clouds, they are where the bright white stops with the inconvenient truth that the bawdy sun has found it's limits. This is where reality sets in. Grandeur becomes reality. Mired in churn.

Below the glow, is where I am as well. There is no brightness, no amount of white added to the mire will make it white. Resentment becomes contempt as I am a proxy for the guilt of others. This is my mire. I am and will continue to be a most convenient villain. Absolve themselves of accountability. Displace it to my detriment. This is my churn. Aching for the glow.

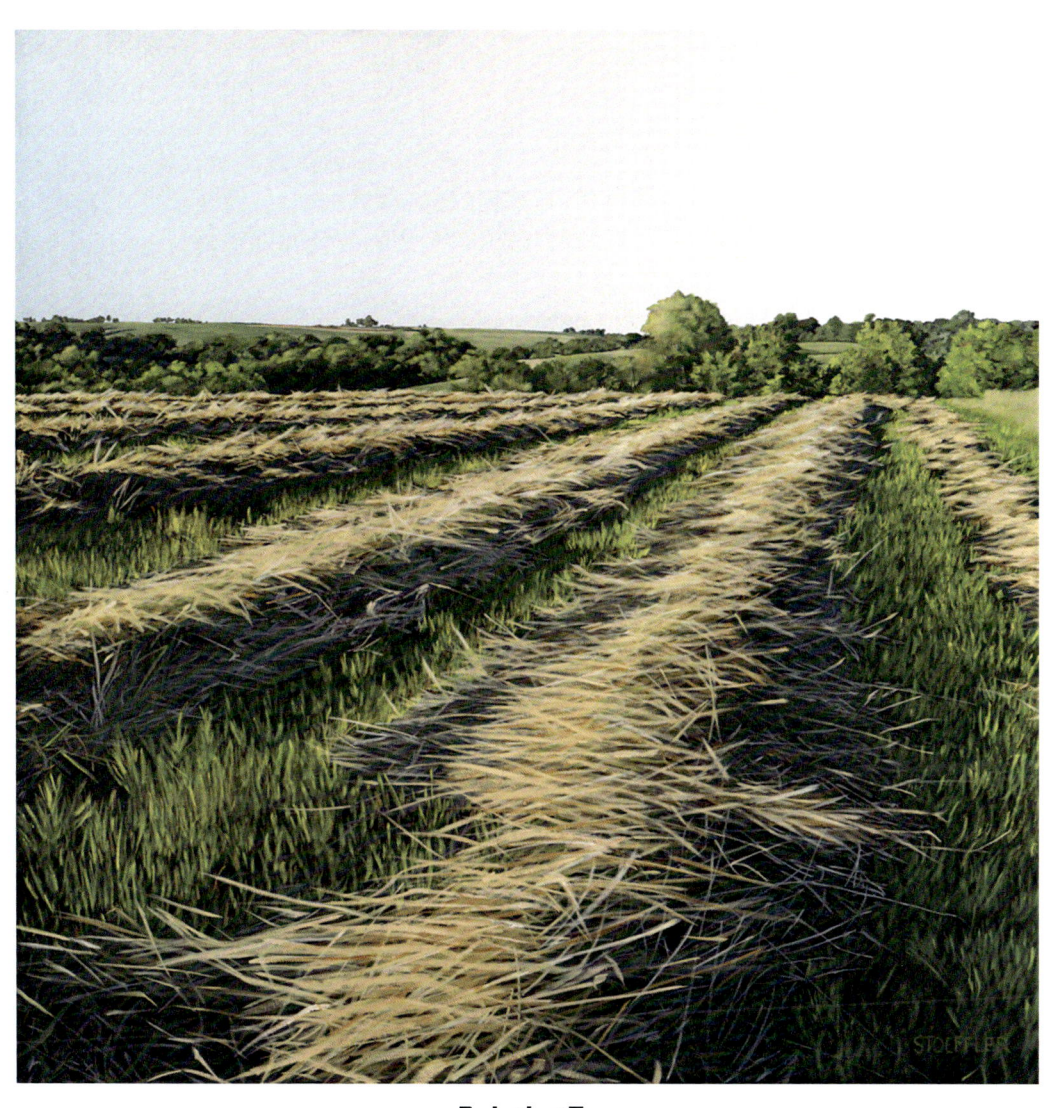

Painting 7

Painting 7: Impressions

ESSAY 7

This was a time of contrasts. This was a time of struggle and joy. With the road humming beneath me I watched the broken collection of tangled clouds race across the fields and forests. Shadows pouring effortlessly down hillsides, through valleys, racing across the steady smooth flats. This was a delightful distraction. These clouds were heavy, dense, dark, and disorganized. Frenetic and unpredictable. Both looming and racing across the sky. Broken only by spaces, creating glorious places, moments of brilliance and warmth. Respites of joy carved through, worn through, the heaviness. Light, escaping, fleeting and golden.

The challenge to navigate between the two. The steely darkness of the clouds was emphasized by the brilliant interruptions. The edges sharper, the darks colder, the weight heavier than if they had simply stitched themselves together into a passive worn grey blanket of worry and doubt, merely a dreary barrier from the unknown glow above. The spaces between highlighted their harshness. It could not be dismissed.

The glow, though, could never feel so immediately warming, be so immediately appreciated and immersive if it were not a deliverance from the steely cold and dark. Not subtle, but quick, like a downpour of soaking sunlight. Drenching warm and gold. This is the same golden warmth that would go unnoticed on a day steeped in sunshine and a cloudless sky. This was the same warmth, but warmer now. This was the same cold, but colder now.

My soul was heavy, dense, dark, and disorganized. Frenetic and unpredictable. My heart looming and racing with trepidation. Where I was. Where I should be. Who I was. Who I should be. Allowances for space between. It was making the darks colder, their edges sharper. The golden warm shining, breaking through, was immediately warming. The lightness that had been hidden was revealed now. The heaviness felt more oppressive now. Pressing. Stubborn. No longer a blanket, but a weight.

The hope was in the spaces between. The warmth was in the spaces between. The joy and the future were in the spaces between. I wanted to expand those spaces. Push the darkness apart to distant places until it had no chance to weave itself into a dark blanket again. Disperse and find their disparate spaces, isolated and predictable. Leave me, drenched in light and hope and the joy of being.

POEM 4

The whole sky

The whole sky
And what was to keep me from immersing myself in that alone
To frame my ambiguous claim of infinite blue and saturate myself in it
To let myself, allow myself, to disconnect completely

Effortless
foregoing orientation
obligation
perspective

What was the weight of my tether
How small was the patch of green that could ground me
What was the value of that restriction
Was there value in that restriction

I knew the value
I knew the weight
as minimal as it could be
It made the sky whole

The question of how much was really how little.
How little did I need for reference
orientation
connection

How little did I need to acknowledge before I could immerse myself
in the vastness of something boundless
Only
enough

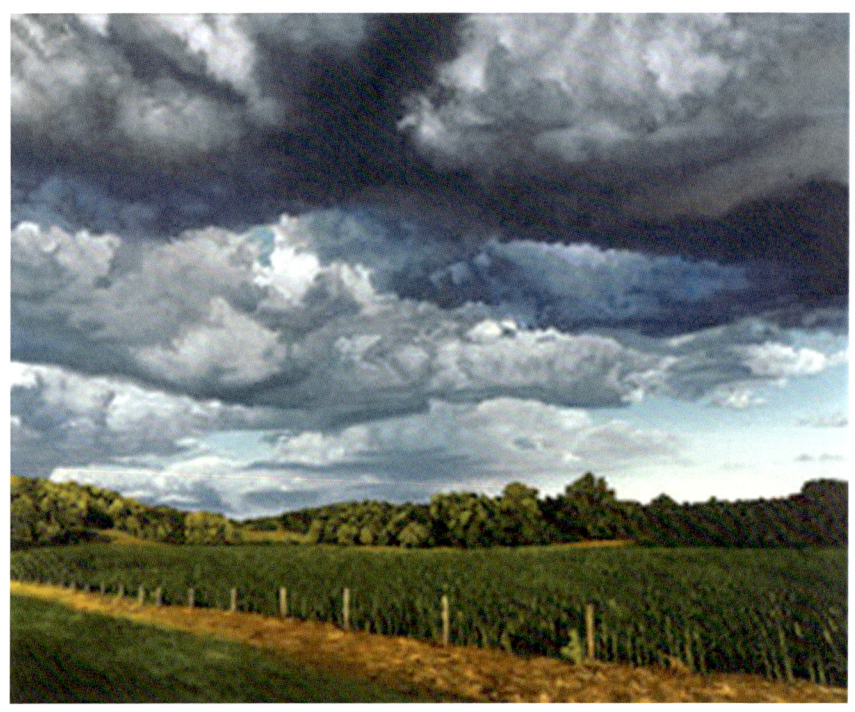

Painting 8

Painting 8: Impressions

ESSAY 4 (2/2)

They had ushered us to a room. It must be busy today, I thought, to be moving people to different rooms. In the tiny room they told us that they had tried to save her, but that they were not going to be able to. They didn't have any answers, but we could be with her while they turned off the machines that were keeping her alive. I was aware of people staring as we moved to the room, but I had no sense of myself. I held on to her and she was warm and I was sure they were mistaken. There was a sound, a horrible sound, and I wondered why they couldn't turn it off like they turned off the machines that were keeping her alive. I realized that the disconnected, untethered, otherworldly sound was me. Wailing. Everything was broken. I was broken. I would never be the same.

She had completely saturated me in love. Her graciousness and love filled my soul completely to overflowing. I didn't want her to leave. I didn't want to watch her leave. I wanted her to stay with me forever and my knowledge of the fleeting nature of life was tugging at my soul. I turned around and I didn't look back. I wanted to remember her as she was.

I set myself toward the dark horizon. The pace of my life was slower now, heavy now. I was careful now to navigate my way. The months that followed were as if only lit by the moon. Absence haunted the cool night air. The distance home would seem farther. Every day a challenge tugging at my bare soul. The depths deeper, still, heavy, and dark. My path felt cumbersome, more treacherous, and long. I kept my pace and let myself feel the loss, dissolving into the deepening sorrow. Alone.

I didn't paint for months. Everything felt broken. There was no inspiration, there was no spark, just darkness and disrepair and I let myself feel it. To go completely through it, aching for the other side.

I was last in line for whose loss this was. I had no place in the reception line, tying everyone together. Untethered.

And then there were stars...

Friendship, bright and brilliant. Filling the deep and empty darkness of me. Illuminating the intricacies and grandeur of these great depths of sorrow. My shining, timeless, constant companions. Reminding me I was not alone, even at this great distance. My home would always be under this canopy of constellations. Reminding me where I am. Who I am. Anywhere and everywhere. My wisdom for the journey forward. Brilliant, steady and strong. Brandished by sorrow to a new shine...because there were stars.

POEM 5

The golden
warm low hum of sun settling to sunset.
Settling soft and heavy with the smell of tea.
Steeping, it softened the edges of every blade,
every leaf,
every petal,
every wing,
every chirp and chatter
Casting a golden spell
Glistened to glow for every green and cream and yellow
Glistened to glow for every flit and flutter
The stems bow and nod slowly
Wings kite and settle
Cool pools to the dark
Steady
Sinks to seeds and roots
Burrows and hollows

ESSAY 8

The trajectory was inward and the distance was infinite. Despite the path before me and the impossible destination I was invested in, immersed in, the journey. Navigating dark and light my only intention was onward.

The clouds encompassing all with a sweeping evolution of sharp to soft. Harsh to harnessing the beauty and boldness of light in a way that allowed both to shine. Once impossibly close, impossibly bright, impossible to see from having captured too much light until stretching, and reaching away, they found the distance needed to subdue the dissonance and make the most of what they had been given, gifted, granted.

The dark grasses swayed and poured from the shadows to spill across the gravel path and rise, bright on the other side. Shining. Stretching to catch the fleeting gold and pull it quick and deep to be claimed and held by their grounding cool tethers. To be claimed and held by the distance, shifting to shade, and creeping to claim the light into darkness.

The path uneven and dappled with ambitious blades and leaves struggling to connect the shadows and the shine. The path worn and uneven, unsteady, unpredictable as it disappears in the distance. Alluding to only the present. No promises, no intentions, no directions, just onward, to the distance.

The distance was an infinite promise. An infinite destination not to be reached. The journey navigating the dark to the light. Navigating the uneven, unsteady and unpredictable. Connecting the shadows and the shine. Capturing the gold and harnessing the light. Pulling it deep. Inward and onward.

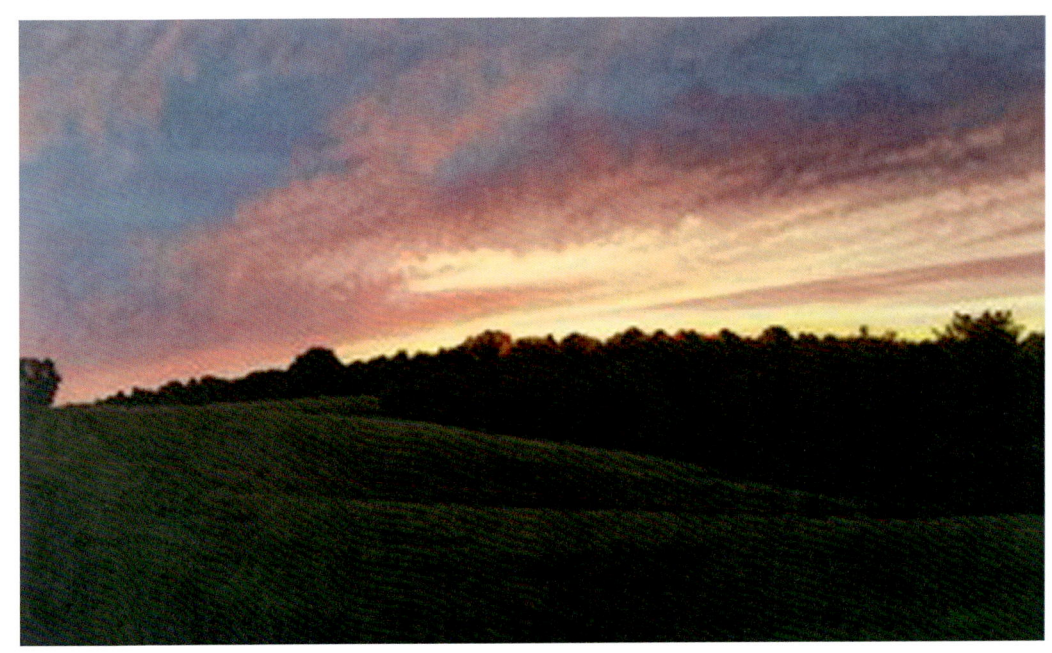

Painting 9

Painting 9: Impressions

ESSAY 9

Every day had felt like a compromise.

Today I stared at the work and let myself not like it. I let myself disagree with the lean of the trees, the cacophony of greens, the unkempt grasses, the unapplied technique, the time not spent, the details dismissed - disregarded.

A long list of compromises on display before me. Promises to myself unkept. Potential unfulfilled. Talent unspent. Beauty unrecognized, unappreciated. Staring back at me from the honest weave of oils on canvas.

The roads that lead me here are harrowing, they snake and drop and heave. Jump creeks and deftly etch through trees with broken light slashing through canopies, then lift to open and reveal this spacious, placid, plain. Tidy and tame. Fields stretching to lay like velvet, draped. Patient. A deep sweet breath. Allowing adoration and space for the light to lay on warm grasses, adorn branches, and rest in long cool shadows.

All to be breathed in, and felt, and heard. All stories to be uniquely told.

Have I been listening? Had the story become a summary. Washing over truths and the untold glories of blades and branches and bales.

Black then. Back to black then. I remember how to begin and this was not a start, and not a finish. I will erase the story with darkness. I will let them grow from the soil again and tell their stories, bloom again, listen to the whispers and be true.

Patiently share the sweetness of their sun-warmed notes on summer breezes. Patiently share their harrowing tales of ravaging winds and rain worn gullies. Patiently share their bold and lacey details as petals capturing light and adorning grasses as summer jewels. Patiently telling their sun-drenched stoic stand of wood against weather, rooted deep to hold and then bared to the elements. Patiently share the obedient bales resting in careful order, dressed in white and nestled in the tall grasses. Patiently listen to each emerald, each olive, and pine speak their turn, then adorn them with the gilded gifts of summer sweetness.

Now breathed in, and felt, and heard. All stories uniquely told. Tales of triumph and bravery, treacherous and beautiful. A recompense accessed and earned. Lived, honest, and owned. Sweetness.

ESSAY 1 (³/₄)

We were having a little girl. I had such a strong sense of her. The little being nesting in my belly. As though radiating out from her was an energy more powerful than the sun itself, so powerful that it extended beyond her and beyond me. It was a remarkable sense. The energy was an unpredictable and uncontainable spark with an overwhelming sense of unlimited potential in a way that felt expansive, uncontrollable, and unhinged because I couldn't wrap my head around it. Expansive and extraordinary. It was so powerful I couldn't get any sense from her otherwise. The more nuanced aspects of her being that would present themselves later as whispers, were outshined at this moment by her extraordinary energy. She was like a light that shone with a blinding brilliance I had never seen, and I had yet to meet her.

A walk on a fall night before the winter that would see her emergence into the world. Walking at night, magical night, to the river, past the woods and back. The air was cool with my sprite in my belly and the magic of fall all around me pulling the energy of growth and abundance deep into the core of all things living to glow like embers through the coming winter, I felt magical. She felt magical.

Eleven years later we are driving through another magical evening, her and I, but this time it is summer at its peak. The air is dense, saturated, warm and sweet, heavy with the smell of rain and wet earth. Massive, humbling storm clouds tower to the south and east of us. Majestic and evolving. Unfolding, unfurling and erupting in the evening sky. Fueled by the golden energy of the setting sun meeting the cool infinite indigo dissolving into a celestial deep. They are magical. They are humbling in their scale.

I am unable to fathom a way to translate them into something representative of their imposing power, glory, and gracefulness.

The scene is so powerful that we pull off the road, her and I. We step out to stand on the rain-soaked earth to view them in the context of the whole brilliant sky. They rule the whole brilliant sky. They are as untethered, ever-changing, and extraordinary as she is. Powerful, undaunted, and graceful as she is. Fueled by the gilded energy of her own experience as it meets the vast, infinite indigo of her joyful, undaunted, unlimited, journey into the unknown. She is magical.

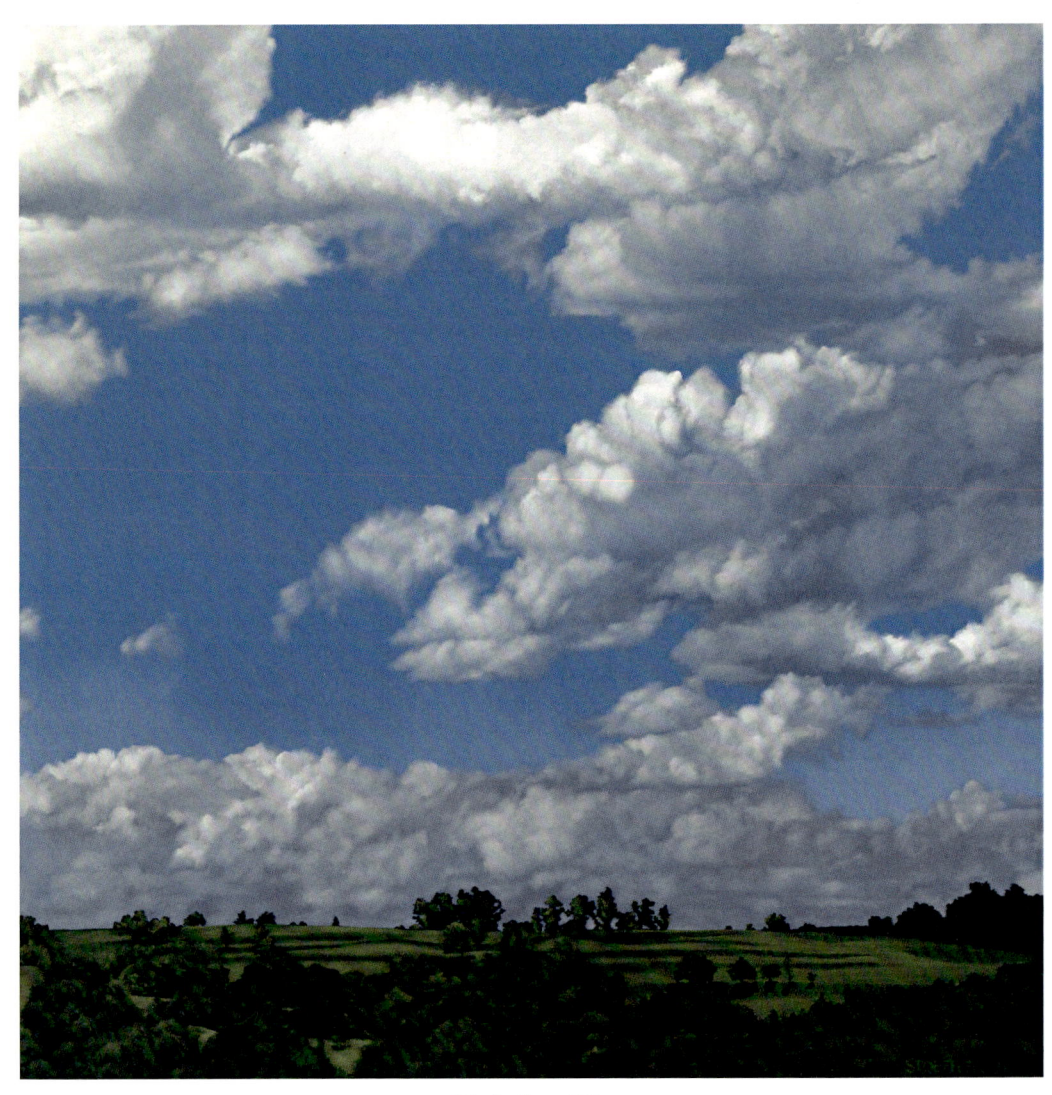

Painting 10

Painting 10: Impressions

THE UNFINISHED EDGES

I was asked to cover these, at least with black, or to pull the image around this artificial bend. But the point at which the plane of the image ends a new world begins. These unfinished edges hold the secrets of the whole painting. The frustrations, the patience, the epiphanies, the problem and the solutions, the innovations, the secrets and the honesty. Uncorrected, unpolished, unapologetic. These edges are my platform for discovery. A palette within a palette unfolding over time. Indigo sky open to the exploration of waves of corals, all the wrong corals until finally the right corals. The journey from hope to discovery. No fear here, just space and more space.

This is where colors are matched for fixing and expanding. This is where directions are explored, to discover what happens when…what ifs…or evens. This is where I learn that sunlight isn't yellow, and shadows are lavender. Pushing colors beyond my assumptions and my expectations to find their truth in the context of their palette. Colors change in the context of the palette. White is not white, grey is not grey, alizarin crimson becomes pink on indigo, periwinkle becomes cool shadows.

The strokes tell the story of patience, frustration, iteration, attempts. Dragging across many worlds to understand those relationships. Variations of push and pull, drag and brush, force and grace. Every time the bristles touch the canvas their response is measured, calculated and controlled, but that calibration lives in the unfinished edges.

To erase these would be to dishonor the struggle and discovery. To disguise the truths that created the vision.

I share my unfinished edges so that my story is complete. Process bare. Journey known.

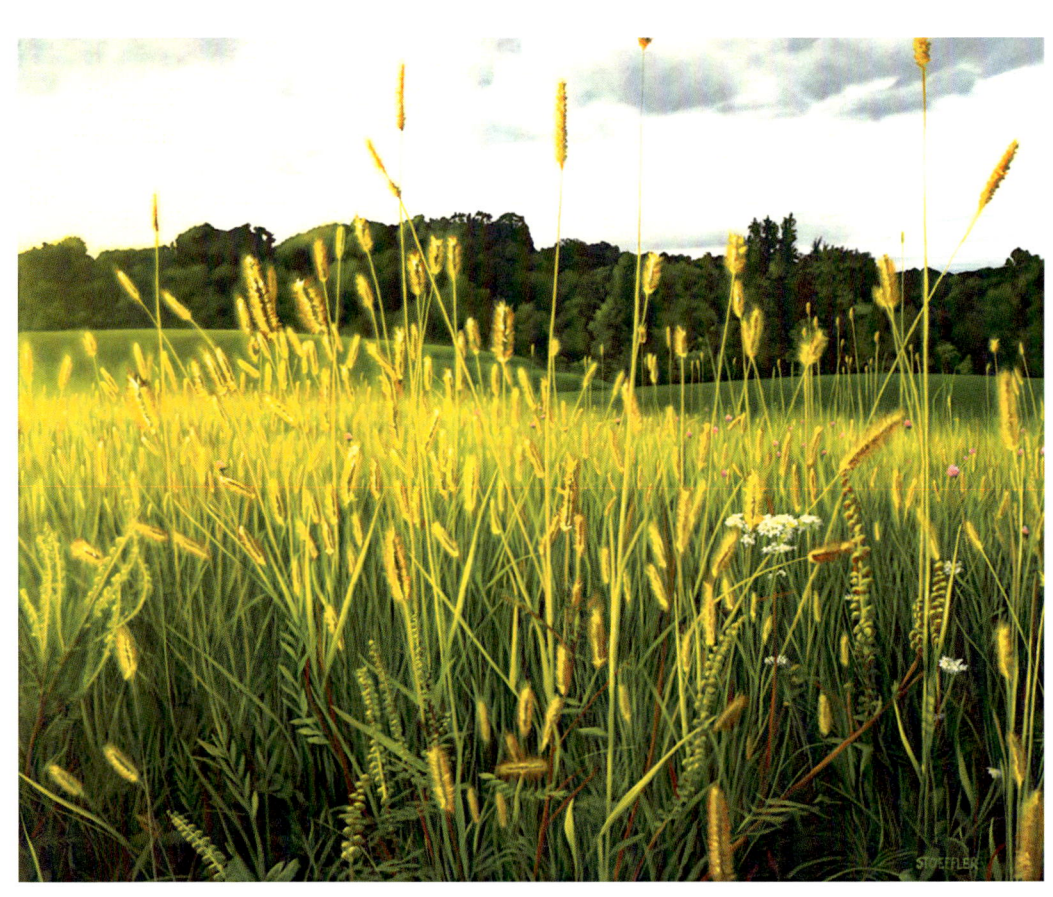

Painting 11

Painting II: Impressions

ESSAY 10

When I first met her she was frail, but mighty. Her small frame resting on cool, crisp white sheets and bathed in the cool steady northern light of the window near her bed. She greeted me with warmth and eagerness. She was the matriarch. I carefully offered my hand in greeting and she took it warmly in hers and held it with both of her small, weathered, and able hands.

Her warm greeting quickly dissolved as her now distracted gaze quickly fell from mine and she turned her attention to my hands in hers. "Your hands, they are so soft," she said with disbelief as she caressed and turned my hands in hers with envy and admiration. Inspecting them from every angle like fine porcelain works of art.

I had not worked the earth as she had. I had not kept animals as she had. I had not kneaded bread daily, as she had. Washed, cleaned, scrubbed daily, as she had. I had not pumped water from the cistern in winter, or drove away coyotes in spring as she had.

But it was my hands that she envied. A simple life, seemingly void of struggle or strife. Familiar with the convenient, sweet, easy warmth of earth as only lawns and meadows. Hands for petting soft purring fur, hands for smoothing soft clean fabrics and linens, hands for coddling warm drinks to stave off cool days. Hands for brushing away spring breeze tousled hair.

I was sad to see the discontent my hands brought her. Her relationship with life was much more intimate than mine. She knew the earth and the seasons in a way that she could cultivate life and sustenance from them. She was self-sustaining in her knowledge and environment, self-reliant, independent in a way few of us will ever be. But it was my hands that she envied. She didn't see the strength, grace, and beauty of her own hands, but I did.

I remembered her hands as I walked on that summer evening, witnessing that glow, gold and warm, slowly simmer with the business of nature settling into the creeping cool. Walking toward the blinding sun, the covering-everything sun. I can't shield my eyes or turn away because the golden warmth on my face, pouring over me, is too indulgent to sacrifice even a sliver of shine. I square my shoulders to the sun, full face to the sun. I walk along the lane along the first hill piece, careful to mind the deep ruts artfully carved into the earth from the recent rain. I let my hand gracefully brush the tops of the grasses, a soft sea of gold swaying in the setting sun. Fragrant and warm and soft. The timothy fires like shooting stars from the surrounding grasses. Explodes into fuzzy golden fireworks that irrationally sway with serendipity at the whim of the breeze. I walk and my hands catch their stems that bow and escape or lead me to their soft tails to delicately admire. And hiding among them, unnoticed, Queen Anne's lace shining its full delicate and detailed face to the sun, hiding below the timothy, but holding court among the alfalfa cool and deep.

Her hands had worked the cool earth, but had they felt it? Her hands had created these fields, these grasses, cultivated these grasses, but did she know these grasses? Did she feel their buoyant softness?

My naive hands have the luxury of appreciating these grasses, they don't know them well enough not to. Were those who worked this land able to have a relationship with these landscapes more intimate than mine. Was it my luxury alone to experience with all my senses this earth and these seasons in a way that I could also create and celebrate the sustenance of them. I was self-sustaining in my admiration for the landscape. Self-reliant and independent in my awareness of it's balance, its beauty, humbled by it's scale. It was these lands that I envied. Maybe she didn't see the beauty in her own lands, but I did.

POEM 6

What it must be like to be light
To expand seemingly infinitely in all directions
always
touching everything
feeling everything
illuminating every thing
And all things reaching to be enlightened
Rescued from the darkness
All things needing to take to give
Until boundaries make hostages -the shadows
Boundaries to limit an otherwise infinite path
A powerful pause
A challenge
What does light make of these boundaries
As obstacle or opportunity
A respite
A reprieve
A resolution
Enough

As I am
Always aching for expansion
Always seeking to share
to shine
to touch every thing
feel every thing
know every thing
Expanding in all directions
Seemingly infinitely
Reaching to be enlightened
Until boundaries take hostages,
make hostages
my shadows
Secrets rescued from the light
Stolen from the shine

a respite
a reprieve
Enough
How will I know these boundaries?
As friends or foe
My obstacles as deliverance
liberation
ransomed from my own ambition
My secrets shadowed
spared, not shared
Sparkle saved, not spent
Self, kept

Can I dissolve into this heavy escape
my rescue
the liberation of my own known boundaries
Can I lay in this field and not ache for what lies beyond it
Can I allow myself steep in the beauty within its known boundaries
Soak the sweet smells deep into me
Still
Let the applause of the canopy hush my ears
Let the bright feathered songs and dizzying whispers of crickets steal
my thoughts
Can I Let my eyes follow the clouds as they build and carefully unfurl to
the deeper blue
out of view
as a welcome mystery
As I am
with known boundaries
Always
Enough

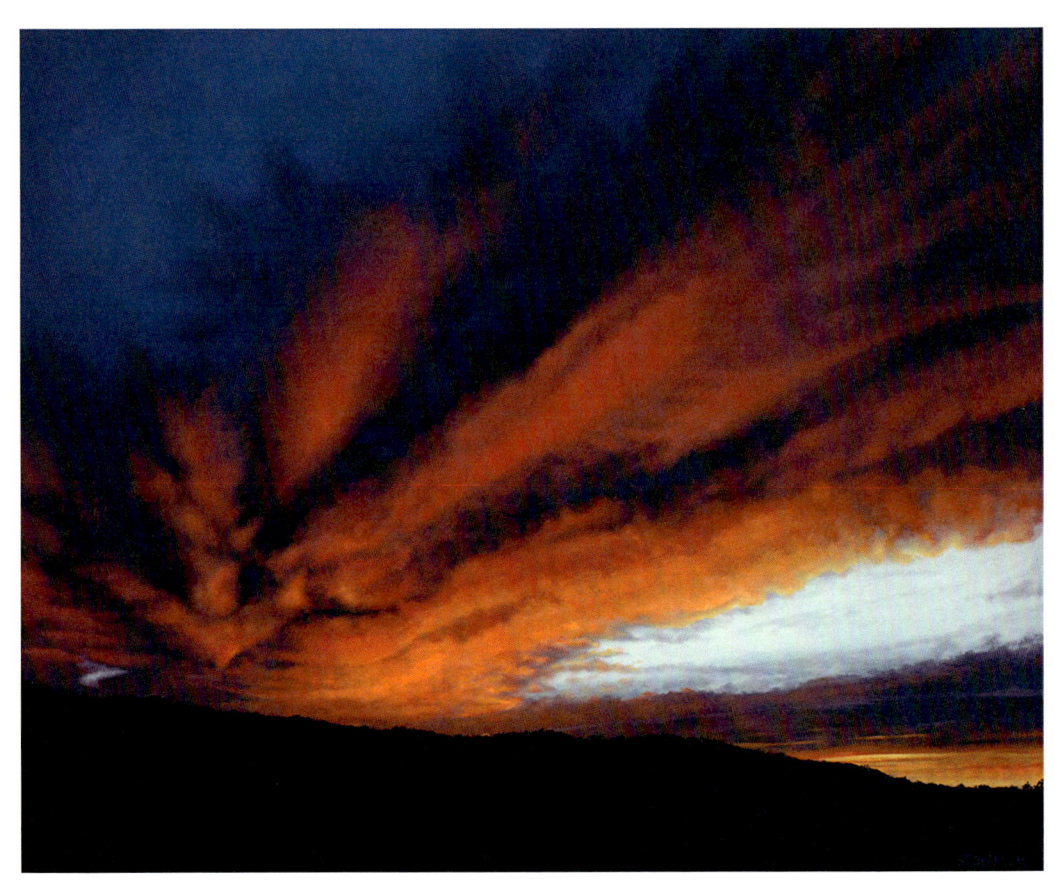

Painting 12

Painting 12: Impressions

ESSAY 11

The sunlight here, sparkling and sparse, was diffused by the canopy adorning the edges of the hollow. It dappled the lush, green flats that settled smooth and calm between the steeps. It was hidden from the cooling pools by the graceful bend and lean of branches. It was glittering on the ripples of the bubbling creek, tripping over smoothed rocks, and glowing warm on the stones set aside by the rise from a previous storm.

The creek carves and sways its way through this fairytale, navigating the deep hollow that winds and guides the wind and water to the river -waiting. Along the creek lush green patches settle in serene spaces between the fortress-like walls that rise to the sky. The green slips from shaded beds beneath branches and leaves, pools and pours down banks to the waiting water, calmly and carefully cloaking the stones in their path. The narrative of the hollow is clear, hushed in soft breezes, lightly applauded by the unstill leaves. Be present, be patient, find and follow your path -no matter how winding.

I witness the stillness. The floor of the Hollow is calm now, smoothed by days and dark nights of high water, powerful, swift, reckless and rushing to the limestone cliffs of Devil's Door. Reshaping without regard, everything in its path. Devil's Door ushering passage to the deep, heavy current of the river, pulling the streams from their beds. The disruptive churn leaving only calm and quiet in its wake. Reshape, recover, reset, reclaim, renew.

And now stillness reigns. Even the light and the air can barely find their way here. Bold colors are woven into the canopy now, a colorful symphony, and serenity prevails. I will listen to every note. The clear, still creek a mirror to admire it's own beauty, a reflection on resilience, of resilience, echoes the celebration. The blue of the sky deepens here to a deceptive depth. Punctuated by displaced stones, the patient water conforms and flows fluidly, seemingly uninterrupted, unaffected by their presence in its slow pour to the river.

I looked back at the second crossing and watched the creek quietly wander through a stand of trees toward me. It was traveling to Devil's Door too. I stood mid-creek, my boots tall enough to stand in the cool water without flooding. The water sparkled around me on its unhurried journey, accepting and enveloping my interruption. I felt still here. Serene and quiet as the warm rocks. Present, patient, finding and following my path -no matter how winding.

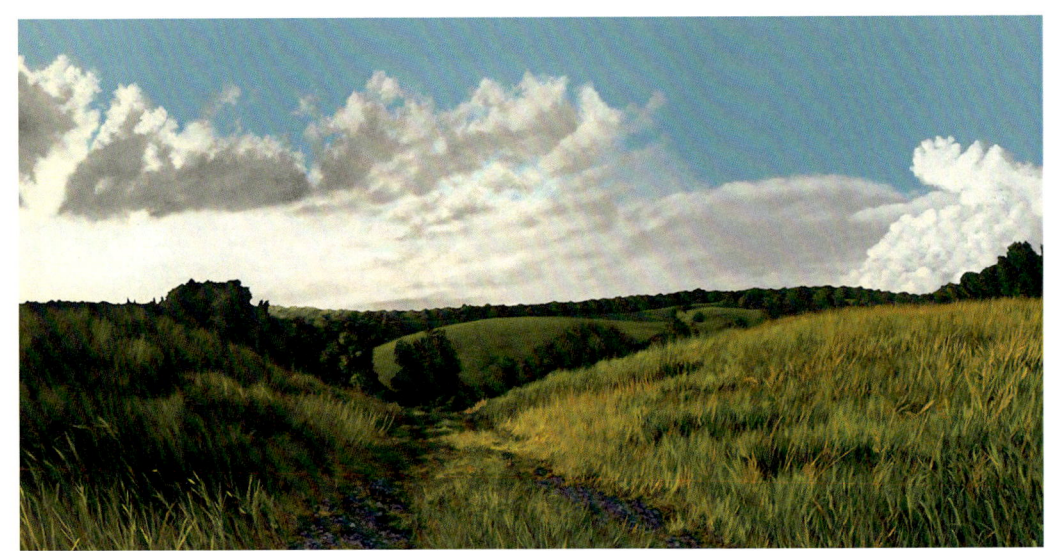

Painting 13

Painting 13: Impressions

ESSAY 1 (4/4)

With the sun to my back and the abyss as their backdrop they swept across the sky. Racing slowly with a constant ease and pace. I would capture them here and honor this moment. Only this single moment. Capturing in pause each plume mid-bloom. Building, growing, glowing. Building each plume in place. Placing plumes on plumes as they unfold, unfurl, and erupt at this single moment. Each plume gilded by the golden gaze of the setting sun, each plume unfolding in place with warm soft edges. Each plume pushing from a cool hidden gray to glorious golden white to feel the fading warmth of the sinking sun before wilting, collapsing, and folding back into itself to fuel the new white to unfold, unfurl, and erupt from the cooling hidden gray. Cycles of regeneration to fuel their evolution.

I watch the whites sink while yellows, and corals and deep lavenders push and creep ever upward, ever bolder, with the setting sun. The clouds race from the sun, their glowing past. They race deftly to the cool deep with certainty, determination, power, and grace, a stark contrast to a star-filled abyss. They race to join the infinite unknown. They don't look back. Never to touch the earth. They race deftly above it, shadowing it deeply with their presence. Knowing, looming, and heavy. They bring darkness, unstoppable. And still visible, when the light finds it, the structure, sealed forever in the infinite indigo.

POEM 7

The shadows could not reach her
They stretched, tangled, long, and dark
They spread, pulling cool from the hollows to steal the sun-warmed grass to shade
They tangled themselves in their efforts, disorganized and desperate
They lengthened themselves, pushed into the fields by the urgency of a settling sun
But the shadows could not reach her
They grasped at blades, building their insufficient arsenal
But the shadows could not reach her
Their reach whittled from heavy branches to tiny twigs, a last gasp, a failed grasp
But the shadows could not reach her
Their wish, to reclaim her from her undeserved independence
Their wish, to suppress her with speckled sunlight and stifled breezes
But the shadows could not reach her
She glowed watching down on them
She glowed watching them try
Bathed in a sun they could not steal and breezes they could not stifle
Her joyful crown and canopy applauded the uninterrupted winds that raced over her ridge
The hay bales adorned her like a golden necklace, strewn
The sweetgrasses swayed, perfumed the bed beneath her deeply rooted feet
Unintended in this fenceline, she stayed, deeply rooted
Out of place among these hay bales, she stayed, deeply rooted
She faced in all directions, her gaze on all horizons, distant and determined
glowing, glorious, gleeful
The forest, envious, loomed near to remind her, reclaim her
Their shadows could not reach her

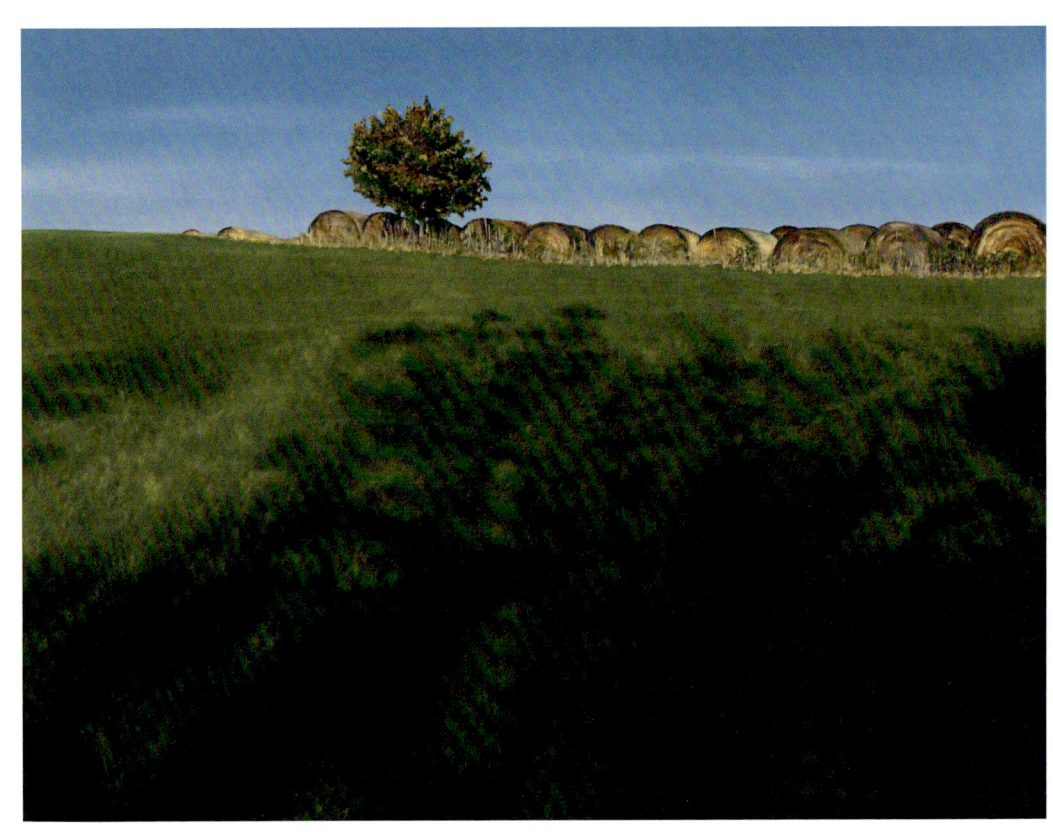

Painting 14

Painting 14: Impressions

POEM 8

Indeed
she didn't belong with the others
but was, regardless, and without regard, bold, beautiful, and bright
telling her story
Petals draped in a velvety pout,
pouring from a crown of emboldened golden, vermilion, alizeron, glory
She knows
She holds her place, owns her beautiful space
Telling her story
The brightness ebbs and flows to tips
caressing the edges
tracing the boundaries
announcing endings and beginnings
Kindly accepting and reflecting the adoring, and adorning, light
Telling her story
And crimson
interrupting to share the heavy secrets of valleys and veins
the interrupted terrains
where the truth pools and pours to streams that fall away
forgotten
Crimson to remind the bright tips of their darkness
Crimson to hold the heavy burden of a light it doesn't share
A light that would steal its depth and betray its truth
Crimson to anchor petals deep and dark and true
with the honest grounding rooted in shadows
Telling her story
Enter the levity of light that makes everything glow
and everyone know the easy, familiar, joyful, brilliance
Variance betrayed by the brightness
subtext subdued
to something simple and smooth
But crimson will not be denied
As angles shift and the lean of light loses its directness
the bloom of crimson seeps from deep and bleeds a bolder story
Crimson creeps in whispers on whites

with hints of something daring
Sweeps to complete spaces
and embraces the indigoes' hiding places
Plays in the shadows with prussians and azures
Telling her story
Her crowning glory
Her defense, a gilded oratory
Of unrushed details expressed and heard
Points bared
Truth tipped
Telling her story
A warning of spikes and daggers
Emboldened, golden, vermilion, alizarin
To listen

The Shadows Could Not Reach Her is Kristin's first book. A study of meaning-making in the form of essays, poems, and paintings. Kristin received her BA in Art from the University of Iowa along with degrees in Psychology and Journalism & Mass Communication. A lifelong artist, Kristin's was born and raised in Iowa and grew up visiting farms in Northeast Iowa, where her family hails from. It was this place, and these people, that inspired her to paint landscapes. "I knew what a traditional landscape should look like, but I hoped that I could paint something that would relay how I felt when I was a part of these landscapes—standing at the crest of the hill, pieces shaded by the giant hay bales, humbled by the massive clouds overhead and great expansiveness of scenery around me. I realized that these landscapes would be different, that these vistas were more powerful than passive, saturated with color, and awe-inspiring in their scale."

Kristin's art is currently represented by Gilded Pear gallery and her piece *Infragilis* was recently selected for the Land/Scape: Climate, the Environment, and Beyond juried exhibition at the Cedar Rapids Museum of Art. Kristin's work can be found in many private and corporate collections and has been included in solo and joint art shows with galleries including The Corner House Gallery and Gilded Pear Gallery. A seasoned learning scientist, she is also currently working on her PhD with the University of Amsterdam with a focus on the definition and measurement of Creative Thinking, Critical Thinking, and Collaborative Problem Solving.

For more information and to see works available for purchase please visit klansing.com, or use QR code:

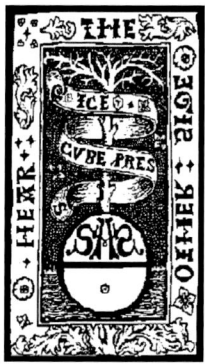

The Ice Cube Press began publishing in 1991 to focus on how to live with the natural world and to better understand how people can best live together in the communities they share and inhabit. Using the literary arts to explore life and experiences in the heartland of the United States we have been recognized by a number of well-known writers including: Bill Bradley, Gary Snyder, Gene Logsdon, Wes Jackson, Patricia Hampl, Greg Brown, Jim Harrison, Annie Dillard, Ken Burns, Roz Chast, Jane Hamilton, Daniel Menaker, Kathleen Norris, Janisse Ray, Craig Lesley, Alison Deming, Harriet Lerner, Richard Lynn Stegner, Richard Rhodes, Michael Pollan, David Abram, David Orr, and Barry Lopez. We've published a number of well-known authors including: Mary Swander, Jim Heynen, Mary Pipher, Bill Holm, Connie Mutel, John T. Price, Carol Bly, Marvin Bell, Debra Marquart, Ted Kooser, Stephanie Mills, Bill McKibben, Craig Lesley, Elizabeth McCracken, Derrick Jensen, Dean Bakopoulos, Rick Bass, Linda Hogan, Pam Houston, and Paul Gruchow. Check out Ice Cube Press books on our web site, join our email list, Facebook group, or follow us on Twitter. Visit booksellers, museum shops, or any place you can find good books and support our truly honest to goodness independent publishing projects and discover why we continue striving to hear the other side.

Ice Cube Press, LLC (Est. 1991)
North Liberty, Iowa, Midwest, USA
Resting above the Silurian and Jordan aquifers
steve@icecubepress.com
Check us out on twitter and facebook
Order direct: www.icecubepress.com
Subscribe to our Substack page:
The Pulse of A Heartland Publisher

Celebrating Over Thirty Years of Independent Publishing

To Fenna Marie—
completely and remarkably the
umbra, penumbra, and antumbra.
A shadow in all its shades
at play amidst the light.